FROM FARM TO YOU

Cheese

Carol Jones

CHELSEA HOUSE
PUBLISHERS
A Haights Cross Communications Company
Philadelphia

This edition first published in 2003 in the United States of America by Chelsea House
Publishers, a subsidiary of Haights Cross Communications.

Chelsea House Publishers
1974 Sproul Road, Suite 400
Broomall, PA 19008-0914

The Chelsea House world wide web address is www.chelseahouse.com

Library of Congress Cataloging-in-Publication Data Applied for.
ISBN 0-7910-7005-0

First published in 2002 by
MACMILLAN EDUCATION AUSTRALIA PTY LTD
627 Chapel Street, South Yarra, Australia, 3141

Copyright © Carol Jones 2002
Copyright in photographs © individual photographers as credited

Edited by Anne McKenna
Text design by Judith Summerfeldt Grace
Cover design by Judith Summerfeldt Grace
Illustration on p. 21 by Pat Kermode, Purple Rabbit Productions

Printed in China

Acknowledgements

The author wishes to thank Richard Thomas of Richard Thomas Cheese for his help with the writing of this book.

Cover photographs: Variety of soft cheeses courtesy of Photolibrary.com/Foodpix, slice of Swiss cheese courtesy of Artville.

APL/Corbis © Adam Woolfitt, p. 6, © Dean Conger, p. 8 (small), © Philip Gould, p. 19 (right), © Owen Franken, p. 21, © Michael St. Maur Sheil, p. 22 (top), © Leonard de Selva, p. 26; The Art Archive/Egyptian Museum Cairo/Dagli Orti, pp. 5, 6 (left); Courtesy of Bega Cheese, pp. 22 (bottom), 23 (top), 25; Charlie and Cathy Cafiso, The Burwood Deli, p. 27; Copper Leife/Craig Forsythe, pp. 9 (small), 28 (France and Lebanon); Corbis Digital Stock, pp. 3 (bottom right), 28 (Italy and England); DW Stock, p. 4; Getty Images/Image Bank, p. 23 (bottom), Photodisc, pp. 3 (top left), 28–9 (map), 28 (Netherlands and Switzerland); Imageaddict, p. 29 (USA); Carol Jones, pp. 3 (bottom left and top right), 10–15; Courtesy of Lactos Cheese, p. 24; Mary Evans Picture Library, p. 7 (right); Photolibrary.com, p. 20, FoodPix, pp. 8–9 (main); Ken Stepnell, pp. 18, 19 (left); Stockbyte, pp. 16–17.

Contents

The world of cheese

In the supermarket dairy case, and behind glass at the delicatessen, you will find a whole world of different cheeses.

There are soft fresh cheeses, hard grating cheeses and mild **processed** cheeses. There are cheeses so strong they smell like old socks. Yet cheese is really just milk with much of the water removed.

The main ingredients in cheese are milk, **rennet**, a **starter culture** and salt. The milk is **coagulated** or curdled to separate the curds from the whey.

Cheese can be made from the milk of many mammals, but most of our cheese comes from cow's, goat's or sheep's milk.

Cheese has been made for thousands of years throughout Europe, North Africa, the **Middle East** and Central and South Asia.

Feta cheese is enjoyed all over the world.

The history of cheese

No one knows exactly when cheese was first made. It may have been more than 8,000 years ago.

Cheese was probably first made by the **nomadic** tribes of Central Asia or the Middle East. They stored milk in pouches made from the stomachs of young animals. As they traveled, the heat made the milk go sour and it coagulated from the natural **enzymes** in the stomach pouches. Some tribes also discovered vegetable substances, such as fig tree sap, curdled milk quickly.

The **Old Testament** of the **Bible** mentions cheese. So does the ancient Greek poet Homer. His famous story of *The Odyssey* tells of the giant one-eyed Cyclops who lived in a cave and made sheep's cheese drained in wicker baskets. Homer describes a cheese similar to the feta still eaten in Greece today.

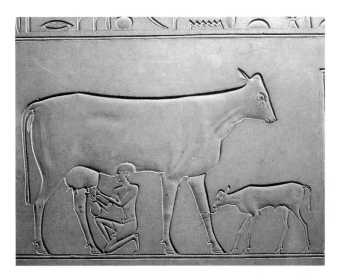

Carvings from ancient Sumer (now Iraq) show the milking of cattle, 5,000 years ago.

Firsts

Pots have been found containing the remains of cheese in a 5,000-year-old Egyptian tomb. These were probably some of the first cheeses.

Many kinds of cheese were sold in the markets of ancient Rome. The Romans took cheese to the British Isles and other places where it was unknown. They also brought back new cheeses to Rome, such as the famous French sheep's milk cheese, roquefort.

Christian Crusaders fighting in the Middle East 1,000 years ago brought back new cheese secrets to Europe. The Vikings who traded and raided in Northern Europe also helped spread knowledge of different cheeses. By the **Middle Ages**, there were famous cheeses being made all over Europe.

Cheese makers in France and Spain have traditionally ripened their cheese in caves.

Strange but true!

In 1841, the Uruguayan navy ran out of cannonballs during their battle with the Argentinian navy. They used Dutch edam cheeses instead!

Cheese was often used to feed armies because it was nourishing and easily transported. The Roman army carried cheese, as did Genghis Khan's warriors when they marched across the world. Travelers to new lands often carried cheese. The first dairy cows arrived with settlers to North America in 1611 and cheese making began there soon after. The first cows arrived in Australia in 1788.

Throughout the world, the secrets of cheese making were passed down in families and monasteries for hundreds of years. It was not until the 1800s that cheese began to be made in factories.

A Byzantine cheese maker from around 400 A.D. on his way to market

Making cheese in a Dutch farmhouse in about 1900

Famous cheeses

The Norwegian cheese gammelost grows a long white mold that looks like fur. The mold is pressed into the cheese and it slowly turns a brownish color.

Kinds of cheese

There are four main kinds of cheese: fresh cheese, soft cheese, firm cheese and hard cheese.

1. Fresh cheeses

Fresh cheeses are very simple. They contain a lot of moisture and are not left to mature, or ripen. Fresh cheeses such as cottage cheese and Indian panir do not keep for very long.

Some soft cheeses ripen or age from the inside. Others, such as the large round brie shown here, ripen from the outside and form a rind.

2. Soft cheeses

Soft cheeses have less moisture than fresh cheese. They are left to ripen for a short time. Camembert and mozzarella are ripened for three to four weeks. Blue-veined cheeses such as gorgonzola are ripened for three months.

Another way of grouping cheese is by the type of milk used. Milk from cows, goats, sheep, buffalo, camels, mares and even reindeer can be used to make cheese. The picture above shows a camel being milked in Mongolia.

3. Firm cheeses

Firm cheeses such as cheddar and gouda have even less moisture than soft cheeses and are left to mature for longer. They are usually ripened from the inside.

4. Hard cheeses

Hard cheeses such as emmental and parmesan have the least moisture of all. They are ripened for up to five years and are often difficult to cut. Because they are so hard, they are excellent for grating.

Cheeses come in many shapes and sizes: wheels, cylinders, blocks, bars, triangles and even pyramids.

Preservation

The great Italian traveler Marco Polo wrote that the Mongols dried skimmed milk out in the sun to preserve it. Even today, the cheeses that last longest are the hardest, driest and saltiest ones, such as the parmesan and grana padano of Italy. They have been known to keep for 100 years.

How cheese is made

Most cheese is made in large factories. There are also many small cheese makers all around the world. Some sell cheese from their own small factories. Others are farmers who make the cheese by hand and sell it to a large cheese company.

The cheese vat is heated by steam.

The cheese makers shown here are making an Italian-style soft cheese called gorgonzola. It has a blue-green mold through it.

Hoops are used to shape the cheese.

Ingredients

To make this cheese, the following ingredients are used:

- milk — delivered from the farm
- rennet — an enzyme (**protein**) taken from a calf's stomach, which coagulates the milk (can also be extracted from yeasts or molds)
- starter culture — a culture of living **bacteria** to **ferment** the cheese, imported from the region where the cheese was first made
- mold culture — also from the region where the cheese was first made
- salt.

Tools and equipment

Most of the tools used to make this cheese are similar to those used for centuries.

Some of the tools used are:

- cheese vat heated by steam
- curd knife — a tool with metal strings used to break up the curd
- draining tables
- spatula
- hoops
- muslin — a type of material
- cheese presses or girdles
- spike.

Method

Preparing the milk

The cheese maker heats milk in the vat to about 150 degrees Fahrenheit (65 degrees Celsius) for 30 minutes to **pasteurize** it. This kills any harmful bacteria. Then the milk is let cool to about 85 degrees Fahrenheit (30 degrees Celsius). Rennet is added to the warm milk to coagulate it. The rennet causes chemical changes in the milk which makes the milk change from liquid to a solid known as curd.

A starter culture of good bacteria is added. Once these bacteria grew naturally in each cheese-making region and got into the milk as it was left standing. The type of bacteria, the grass that the cows ate and the local climate combined to give each cheese its taste. Now bacteria culture is deliberately added.

The milk is left for another 30 minutes until it sets to a junket (a milky jelly), and for the bacteria to grow.

The cheese maker pours rennet into the vat.

Checking the junket with a spatula to see whether the milk has set enough for cutting

Cutting the curd

When the milk has set, a curd knife is cut through the junket several times to allow a watery liquid called whey to separate from the curd. Soft cheeses such as gorgonzola are cut gently into big globs. Hard, dry cheeses are cut finely into pieces as small as rice grains.

After resting for 15 minutes, the junket is stirred gently to disturb the curd. This is repeated after another 15 minutes. The cutting and stirring breaks up the curd and takes out moisture.

Cutting the junket with the curd knife

Draining the whey

Cloths are placed on the draining tables and some of the whey is tipped from the vat. Then the curds are ladled into the draining tables and the whey runs off onto the floor and down a drain. The curd drains for 30 minutes.

Stirring the junket with two large metal bowls

Shaping the cheese in hoops

At this stage, the cheese makers drip a liquid blue-green mold into the curd. This living mold is what will give the gorgonzola cheese its blue vein. Then the drained curds are gently lifted into sections of plastic pipe lined with muslin. These are called hoops. The curds will stay in the hoops for 24 to 36 hours, and they are turned every so often. The cheese will shrink by about one-third as the moisture drains out.

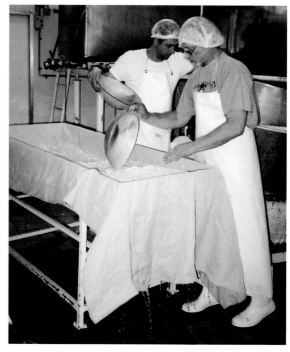

Ladling the curds into the draining tables

Pressing and salting the cheese

After hooping, the cheese is salted on the outside and placed into presses or girdles that can be tightened. The salt reduces the moisture content, adds flavor, helps preserve the cheese and dries the outside of the cheese to form a rind. The cheese will be salted twice over two days.

Salting the cheeses

Maturing the cheese

After salting, the cheese is taken to an air-conditioned maturing room to develop its flavors. With a blue cheese such as gorgonzola, holes are made in the cheese with a steel spike after a week. The holes allow air into the cheese so that the mold will grow.

Cheeses are turned upside down and washed with salty water once a week. After eight to ten weeks, the cheese will be mature. Threads of mold will have grown through the cheese. It will have a thin rind and a soft, almost runny texture inside.

Spiking the cheese

The cheese maker puts the cheeses in the maturing room

Cheeses ripening in the maturing room

The cheese factory

Most of the cheese we eat is made from cow's milk. Many kinds of cheese are made in large **automated** factories. One of the most popular is cheddar cheese.

From farm to consumer

Follow the flowchart to see how milk is processed and made into cheese in large factories, and then transported to stores for sale to the **consumer**.

Read more about each stage of the cheese-making process and how cheese is marketed and sold on pages 18 to 27. Look for the flowchart symbols that represent each stage of the process.

Dairy farming
Milk comes from dairy cows. Farmers use machines to milk the cows.

Packaging the cheese
Packaging materials may be made elsewhere and delivered to the cheese factory. Cheese is cut and packed at the cheese factory.

Transport and storage
The finished cheese is loaded onto **pallets** to be transported by truck to stores or ports.

Transport and storage
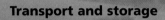
The milk for cheese making is taken by tanker from the farm to the cheese factory.

Processing the milk
At the cheese factory, the milk is cleaned and pasteurized to kill any bacteria. It is heated and then allowed to cool.

Manufacturing cheddar cheese
Large cheese factories use automated machinery to produce cheese and get it ready for packaging.

Transport and storage
The milk is pumped through the cheese factory in pipes.

Marketing and selling cheese
Cheese can be sold locally or exported to other countries.

Buying cheese
The consumer can buy cheese from supermarkets or delicatessens. It should be wrapped and stored in the refrigerator. Harder cheeses keep the longest.

The milk used in large factories to make cheese comes from dairy cows. Dairy cows need rich pasture for grazing. Dairy farmers milk the cows with machines.

Dairy farms need plenty of rain to grow lush pasture. In drier areas, water from dams and rivers is used for irrigation. Some common types of dairy cattle are the jersey, guernsey, holstein and shorthorn breeds.

Pasture is a mixture of grass and other plants such as clover. Farmers may also feed cows grains or hay. In cold climates, cows often spend the winter in barns.

Dairy cows ready for milking

Dairy farm workers
Farmers
Farm hands
Transport workers

Transport and storage

Each day a special truck called a milk tanker collects milk from dairy farms. Milk tankers carry the milk in huge stainless steel tanks. They deliver the milk to the local milk or cheese factory.

Dairy cattle are usually milked twice a day. They need to be milked because their udders become full and heavy. The farmer attaches a hose to the udders which sucks out the milk. A pipe takes the milk to a tank, called a vat, to be cooled and stored. The cows then return to their pasture or barn until the next milking.

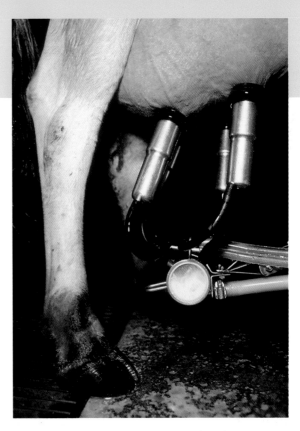

A mechanical milker attached to a cow's udder

Machines are used to milk cows on modern dairy farms.

Tanker drivers take samples of the milk to be tested at the factory to make sure it is fresh and safe.

Conservation

Milking machines and milking sheds must be kept very clean. The run-off water from cleaning the sheds and machines contains detergents, manure, dirt and urine. Some dairy farmers store the run-off in special ponds that contain helpful bacteria to break down the wastes. The pond water or effluent can then be used to fertilize the pastures.

Milk for cheese making is usually taken directly to the cheese factory from the farm. Milk for drinking is taken to a milk factory.

Before cheese making begins, the milk is pasteurized to kill any harmful bacteria. First the milk is pumped through fine cloth filters to remove any dust or dirt. Then it is pumped into vats so big they can hold as much milk as a small swimming pool. The milk is heated to 161 degrees Fahrenheit (72 degrees Celsius), then allowed to cool.

A pasteurizing plant such as this one kills germs by pumping milk over hot stainless steel plates.

Transport and storage

Milk from the farm is tested for bacteria and to find out its fat content. It is pumped into a large stainless steel storage tank. Milk is pumped throughout the factory in stainless steel pipes.

Milk for drinking is usually **homogenized**. This means it is forced through tiny holes to break up the fat and spread it evenly through the milk. Milk for some cheeses, such as processed cream cheese, is also homogenized. Other cheeses are made from milk where the fat content is **standardized**. This can be done by skimming off some of the milk fat (cream) or adding more.

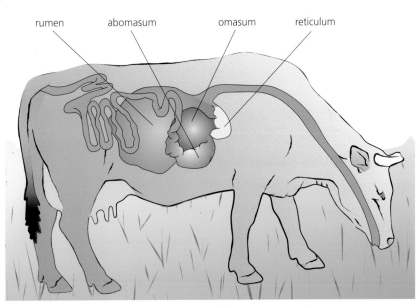

rumen   abomasum   omasum   reticulum

A cow has four stomachs.

Milk tankers deliver milk to the cheese factory for processing.

Strange but true!

Cows have four stomachs. The chewed grass passes through the first two stomachs (rumen and reticulum). Then the ball of grass, or cud, moves back into the cow's mouth. It is chewed another 40 to 60 times before passing through the last two stomachs (omasum and abomasum). Cows actually chew for eight hours, or about 40,000 times, a day!

Processing workers

Production-line workers

Food technologists

Food scientists

Engineers

Transport workers

Large cheese factories use very expensive machines that produce tons of cheese every day. Cheddar cheese is one cheese that is often made in these large factories.

The pasteurized milk is pumped into huge cheese vats. From smaller tanks, starter culture and rennet are added to the milk. Once the milk sets into a junket, the curds and whey are cut and stirred mechanically for about two hours, then heated again slowly to about 98 degrees Fahrenheit (37 degrees Celsius). This second heating helps shrink the curds and removes even more moisture.

Stirring the curds

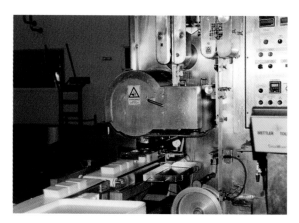

Cheese moving through the factory on a conveyor belt

Manufacturing workers

Cheese maker

Food scientists

Food technologists

Production-line workers

Engineers

Transport and storage

In a fully automated cheese factory, the cheese is pumped through the factory when in liquid form. In solid form it is moved on **conveyor belts**.

Compressing and cutting the cheese

The mixture is then pumped to another machine to be cheddared. During cheddaring, the remaining whey is drained from the cheese curds. A combination of heat and the weight of the curds makes them stick together. The blocks of curd are mechanically stacked and turned over and over again to give the cheese its cheddar texture.

After cheddaring, the curds are milled or cut into finger-sized pieces. Salt is added in a rotating drum. After 20 minutes, the salted curds are sucked by vacuum to block-forming towers. Here the cheese is **compressed** under its own weight. At the bottom of the tower, large blocks of cheese are pushed out into plastic bags. They are then checked, weighed and sealed.

The cheese is cooled and stored at about 46 degrees Fahrenheit (8 degrees Celsius) while it matures. This can take from three to 24 months.

Cheddar cheese compressing tower

Cheese may be matured in large, wheel-shaped blocks coated in wax.

The finished blocks of cheese are sealed in plastic bags, packed in cardboard boxes and stacked on pallets for maturing in a cool room.

Additives

As well as ingredients such as nuts and dried fruit, cheese (particularly processed cheese) may have **additives** such as:

- vegetable colorings
- spices and other flavorings such as vinegar
- **emulsifiers** to make the cheese easier to blend.

23

Cheddar cheese may be made, cut, packed and transported to stores, shipping ports or directly to other food **manufacturers**.

Cheese from large factories is often processed to keep it fresh without refrigeration. To process cheese, one or more kinds of cheese are blended with other ingredients and passed to a cooker where the mixture is heated and stirred. The hot cheese is poured into foil-wrapped blocks, jars or wrapped in plastic film for slices.

Cheese is packaged at the cheese factory.

Transport and storage

After being packaged in plastic, cheese is conveyed to a packing area where it is packed in cartons and loaded onto pallets. Natural cheese is kept refrigerated. Processed cheese does not need refrigeration.

For cheese slices, hot cheese is wrapped in a ribbon of plastic film. It passes through a chilled water bath, the edges are pinched together and the strip is cut into individual slices. The slices are stacked and moved by conveyor belt to be wrapped in outer packaging.

Natural and processed cheese may also be cut into small blocks for sale in supermarkets or large blocks for sale to customers such as food manufacturers. Block cheddar cheese is usually **vacuum-packed**. The company's own brand design may be featured on the packaging, or the brand design of the customer.

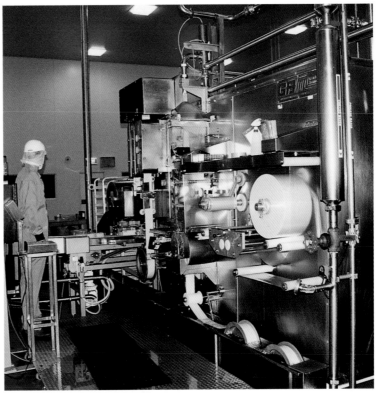

Cheese slices being wrapped in plastic

Packaging plant workers
Production-line workers
Graphic designers
Engineers
Transport workers

The pallets are transported by truck to supermarkets or to large customers such as other food manufacturers. Some cheese will go to a port to be shipped overseas.

Cheese is sold locally or it is exported to other countries. Cheese companies use advertising to encourage consumers to buy their product.

Workers, called merchandisers, from the cheese companies visit stores to make sure that they are receiving the kinds and amounts of cheese they need. They also organize special displays and tastings to help advertise their company's products.

Large cheese companies also advertise their products to a larger audience. They might place advertisements in magazines or on television. Some companies have their own websites to tell consumers about their products.

An advertisement for camembert cheese

Some cheese is displayed in the dairy case at the supermarket. Processed cheese can be displayed on shelves without refrigeration. Many consumers buy farmhouse cheeses or cheese cut to size from a block or wheel. These are usually sold in delicatessens. Supermarkets have their own delicatessens that sell these cheeses.

Consumers can choose from a huge range of hard, soft and fresh cheeses at their local supermarket or delicatessen. Cheeses can be used in salads, on savory dishes such as pizzas, on sandwiches — or simply eaten alone.

Delicatessens cut cheese to suit the consumer's needs.

Marketing and sales workers

Merchandisers

Shelf-fillers

Checkout operators

Bakers

Graphic designers

Copywriters

Home storage

Cheese should be stored in the refrigerator unless you live in a very cold climate. Wrap cheeses separately in greaseproof paper or plastic film. The harder the cheese, the longer it will keep. Fresh cheese such as ricotta should be eaten within a week of purchase. Cheese is best served at room temperature.

Cheese around the world

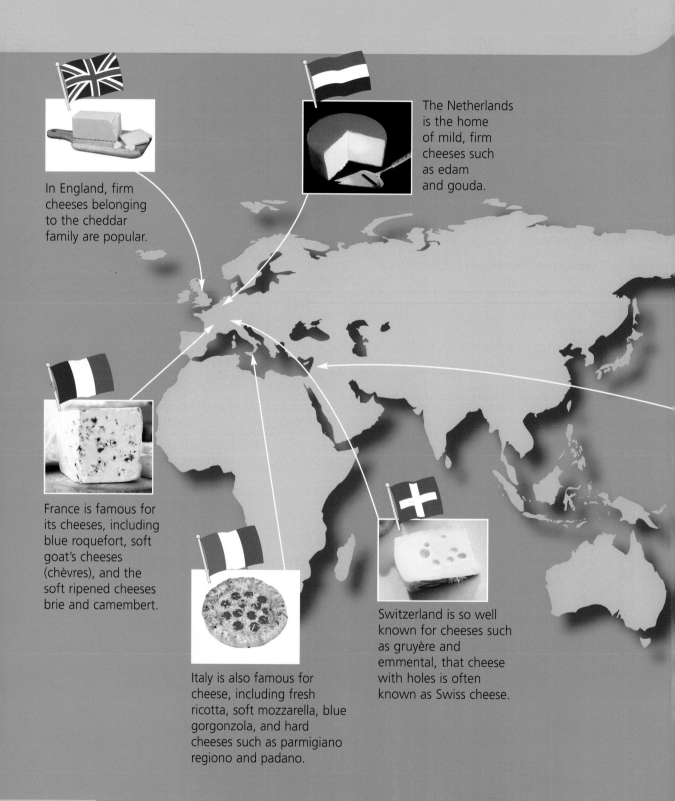

In England, firm cheeses belonging to the cheddar family are popular.

The Netherlands is the home of mild, firm cheeses such as edam and gouda.

France is famous for its cheeses, including blue roquefort, soft goat's cheeses (chèvres), and the soft ripened cheeses brie and camembert.

Italy is also famous for cheese, including fresh ricotta, soft mozzarella, blue gorgonzola, and hard cheeses such as parmigiano regiono and padano.

Switzerland is so well known for cheeses such as gruyère and emmental, that cheese with holes is often known as Swiss cheese.